IF THE TABLOIDS ARE TRUE WHAT ARE YOU?

POEMS & IMAGES

MATTHEA HARVEY

GRAYWOLF
PRESS

This publication is made possible, in part, by the voters of Minnesota through a Minnesota State Arts Board Operating Support grant, thanks to a legislative appropriation from the arts and cultural heritage fund, and through grants from the National Endowment for the Arts and the Wells Fargo Foundation Minnesota. Significant support has also been provided by Target, the McKnight Foundation, Amazon.com, and other generous contributions from foundations, corporations, and individuals. To these organizations and individuals we offer our heartfelt thanks.

Published by Graywolf Press
250 Third Avenue North, Suite 600
Minneapolis, Minnesota 55401

www.graywolfpress.org

Published in the United States of America
Printed in Canada

ISBN 978-1-55597-684-2

2 4 6 8 9 7 5 3 1
First Graywolf Printing, 2014

Library of Congress Control Number: 2013958016

Cover and interior design: Sarah Gifford
Cover and interior art: Matthea Harvey

Book design and composition by Sarah Gifford. Display type set in Akzidenz Grotesk, News Gothic, and Titling Gothic; reading text set in Requiem. Manufactured by Friesens on acid-free, 30 percent postconsumer wastepaper.

FOR
DAVID
&
MARGARETE

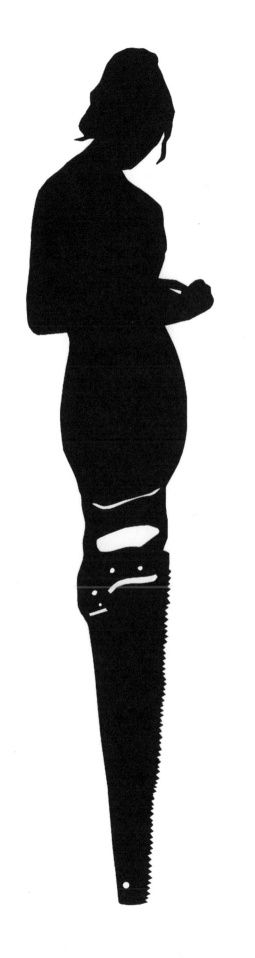

THE STRAIGHTFORWARD MERMAID

The Straightforward Mermaid starts every sentence with "Look…" This comes from being raised in a sea full of hooks. She wants to get points 1, 2 and 3 across, doesn't want to disappear like a river into the ocean. When she is feeling despairing, she goes to eddies at the mouth of the river and tries to comb the water apart with her fingers. The Straightforward Mermaid has already said to five sailors, "Look, I don't think this is going to work," before sinking like a sullen stone. She's supposed to teach Rock Impersonation to the younger mermaids, but every beach field trip devolves into them trying to find shells to match their tail scales. They really love braiding. "Look," says the Straightforward Mermaid. "Your high ponytails make you look like fountains, not rocks." Sometimes she feels like a third gender, preferring primary colors to pastels, the radio to singing. At least she's all mermaid: never gets tired of swimming, hates the thought of socks.

THE HOMEMADE MERMAID

The Homemade Mermaid is top half pimply teenager, bottom half tuna. This does not make for a comely silhouette, and the fact that her bits are stitched together with black fishing wire only makes the combo more gruesome. The Homemade Mermaid floods *Mermag*'s "Ask Serena" column with postcards that read, "O why not half salmon or half koi?" signed Frankenmaid. Sure, she's got the syndrome—loves her weird-eyed maker who began his experiments with Barbies and goldfish in a basement years ago—but she does sometimes wish he'd picked her prettier sister and left her tanning on tinfoil in the yard. When he lugs the Homemade Mermaid to the ocean, she always comes swimming back, propelled only by her arms. She really hasn't reconciled with that tail. The next day he can usually be cajoled into playing a game of All Girl—they tuck her tail in a tank behind her and her human half sits pertly at a desk. Whether she's playing secretary or schoolgirl, the game always ends when the mixture of glue and glitter that he's still perfecting for her tail sparkles gets stuck in the tank ventilation system and the engine coughs to a stop. She sighs as he scoops out the glittery sludge. Tonight again he'll serve her algae with anchovies and she won't complain. The one time he brought her fries—delicious fries—she took them as if in a trance, and dipped them, two at a time into the ketchup. The shared memory sprang to both their faces—two severed legs, blood everywhere, and his hand gripping the saw.

THE INSIDE OUT MERMAID

The Inside Out Mermaid is fine with letting it all hang out—veins, muscles, the bits of fat at her belly, her small gray spleen. At first her lover loves it—with her organs on the outside, she's the ultimate open book. He can pump her lungs like two bellows and make her gasp; ask her difficult questions and study the synapses firing in her brain as she answers to see if she's lying; poke a pleasure center in the frontal lobe and watch her squirm. Want to tug on her heartstrings? No need for bouquets or sad stories about his childhood. He just plucks a pulmonary vein and watches the left ventricle flounder. But before long, she starts to sense that her lover, like all the others before him, is getting restless. This is when she starts showing them her collections—the basket of keys from all over the world, the box of zippers with teeth of every imaginable size—all chosen to convey a sense of openness. As a last resort, she'll even read out loud the entries from her diary about him to him. But eventually he'll become convinced she's hiding things from him and she is. Her perfect skin. Her long black hair. Her red mouth, never chapped from exposure to sun or wind, how she secretly loves that he can't touch her here or here.

THE IMPATIENT MERMAID

hates the slow creep forward of high tide and low tide's slow creep back. She has a twitch in her tail, an itch in her armpits, and a habit of chewing her lips until they bleed, which makes the sharks swarm, then shy away, because of a tiresome but age-old truce with the merfolk. As a child, the Impatient Mermaid was famous for shooting a baby octopus like a slingshot across the ocean floor, then begging for more. Terrible for Underwater Relations. These days, her sisters trail cruise ships, hunting for orange prescription bottles that might be bobbing in the ship's wake. A scallop stuffed with Xanax can give them precious hours of peace. Tick, tock, the moon is a too-slow clock. If the Impatient Mermaid had her way, the moon would zip around the night sky making the ocean all tsunamis and squalls, tipping over ships and whipping the seagulls into a frenzy. She wants shipwrecks and lovers yesterday, and preferably a flipbook fable of her own that has nothing to do with legs—a beautiful blur of her on fastforward, racing a sailfish to a distant distant shore. Truth is, the Impatient Mermaid doesn't want things faster, she wants them finished. She can't wait for the day when the buzzing in her head turns to black and she's dead.

THE TIRED MERMAID

The Tired Mermaid wishes for once her horoscope would just read: hungover today, stay in bed. Instead it feeds her false futures and she starts each new day expecting to finally shine up her trident or compose a ship-sinking shanty. Too much Chianti and none of these things get done. The sun is a blade in the eye that hurts her seaweedy head and doesn't help her stomach, roiling with bits of broken reef. While she's contemplating brushing her teeth, the other mermaids go swishing off to Watercolor Class. The trick is to use a primer of crushed pearls for a spectacular under-sheen when the drawing's dry. Later they'll hold the paintings underwater and see which one fish try to swim into. Fish are efficient judges that way and no one holds it against them. If they're fooled, they're fooled. There's always another day. The Tired Mermaid grimaces, then sneezes. Another day is precisely the problem. It's time to get up. For a jolt of caffeine, she bites an electric eel, and the chill in her molars isn't much, but it's something.

THE MORBID MERMAID

The Morbid Mermaid is drawn to maggots as if by a magnet. If she's not watching things disintegrating underwater, she can be found crouching on the shore, with her head bent over something dead or dreamily watching rain pockmark the ocean. Instead of wearing garlands of living sea-flowers and shrimp, she bobby-pins dead flies and centipedes to her dyed-black hair, giving her silhouette a nubbly look. Mermen have tried courting her with flailing half-dead seals, but to no avail. They're doomed to fail. Death is the lover she longs for. Mer-funerals are the worst since, poof, the merfolk just morph into seafoam. But she circles the days before their dying, making the other mermaids whisper, "Yuck, the necrophiliac's back." Eating the living is how they feed their singing. They shudder when she gulps down a week-old herring she's left to rot on a rock. They can't see that there's something beautiful about a true ending, which is why (apart from the obvious technical difficulties) they don't much like movies, don't read books. She pities the foolish optimists. They'll never know the joy of winding up a metronome, setting it on a rock, then watching its ticking come to a stop.

THE BACKYARD MERMAID

The Backyard Mermaid slumps across the birdbath, tired of fighting birds for seeds and lard. She hates those fluffed-up feathery fish imitations, but her hatred of the cat goes fathoms deeper. That beast is always twining about her tail, looking to take a little nip of what it considers a giant fish. Its breath smells of possible friends. She collects every baseball or tennis ball that flies into her domain to throw at the creature, but it advances undeterred, even purring. To add further insult to injury it has a proper name, Furball, stamped on a silver tag on its collar. She didn't even know she had a name until one day she heard the human explaining to another one, "Oh that's just the backyard mermaid." "Backyard Mermaid," she murmured, as if in prayer. On days when there's no sprinkler to comb through her curls, no rain pouring in glorious torrents from the gutters, no dew in the grass for her to nuzzle with her nose, not even a mud puddle in the kiddie pool, she wonders how much longer she can bear this life. The front yard thud of the newspaper every morning. Singing songs to the unresponsive push mower in the garage. Wriggling under fence after fence to reach the house four down which has an aquarium in the back window. She wants to get lost in that sad glowing square of blue. Don't you?

THE OBJECTIFIED MERMAID

The photographer has been treating her like a spork all morning. "Wistful mouth, excited tail! Work it, work it!" He has no idea that even fake smiling spreads to her eyes and her tail and there's nothing she can do about it short of severing her spine. Without asking, the assistant resprays her with glycerine. It's gonna be hell getting all that grease off her scales tonight but she can't scum up her tank at the bar—its weekly cleanings seem more like monthly these days, and fewer and fewer patrons have been inviting (read: paying) her for a Tankside Mertini and quick feel of her tail. There's one regular who lapses in and out of consciousness and he's the real reason she stays. Every once in a while he seems to have forgotten where he is and he looks at her with the kind of wonder she imagines her grandmother inspired when she first risked coming ashore. After an hour under the studio spotlights, she's starting to smell pretty fishy. Can't blame it (as she has before) on her standard seaweed bra because this fool of a photographer has her holding two clear fishbowls in front of her breasts so it looks like goldfish are swimming past her nipples. She's supposed to pretend it tickles. She wants to ask if he's heard the phrase "gilding the lily" which she recently learned at Land Berlitz. When asked if she's tired, she lies. A downward spiral means the opposite up here.

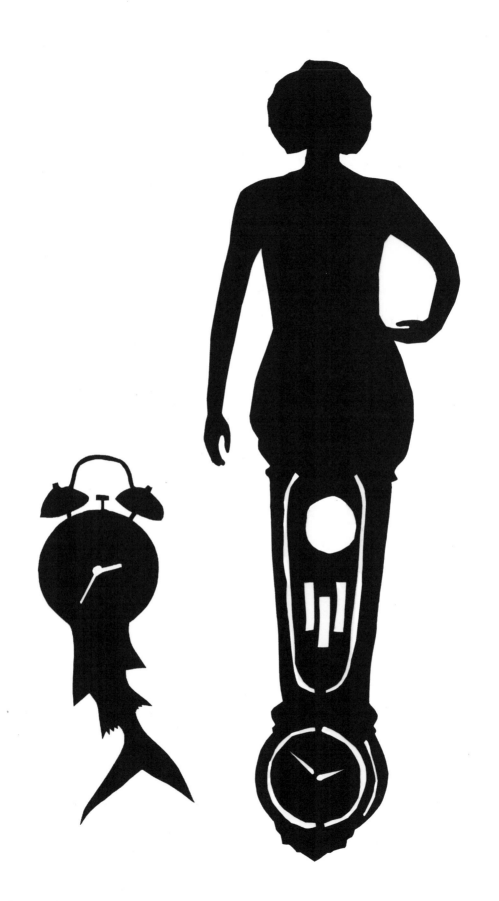

THE DEADBEAT MERMAID

The Deadbeat Mermaid would have done better in a world with rules. Red for stop; green for go. Tea at four and bed at nine. Detention, suspension, wash your face of grime. In the loosey-goosey ocean there's nothing and no one to stop her. It's her Barcalounger with built-in wave massage. She stubs her cigarettes out in the water and by sunset she's usually sporting a soggy beige hula hoop of butts, unless a speedboat zips by and clears the area. The Deadbeat Mermaid left her seven merpups with their merfather years ago, saying, "If seahorses can do it, so can you. Take the Filets out to play." He's no great shakes but he does teach them how to crack open a crayfish and suck out the head. The elegant octopus and tasty squid steer clear of her sludgy surrounds, but for food, she's just as happy with the tourists' leftovers, those soggy parcels of fish and chips wrapped in newspaper that go floating by. The news is blurred and over by the time the paper gets to her, but she doesn't care. Between meals, the Deadbeat Mermaid floats on her back and watches the giant sky, stuck on the same stupid cloud channel all day long.

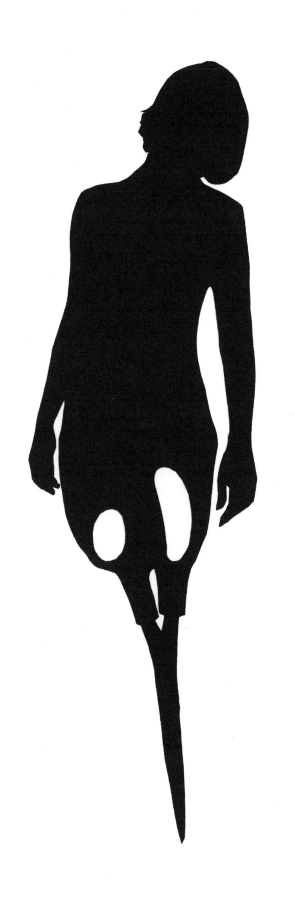

M
Is for
Martian

we
went to school

on

rockets.

the sun

a

dim

formula-the moon in half the Atlantic ... only, now now ... ... or each corner shining to ... ... **I heard** ...

I rushed to the window and stuck my head out.

"Okay, ..."

"Hey!" shouted Ralph Priory. "We just heard ... new schedule today! The Moon job, the one with the new Atto-motor, is cutting gravity in an *hour!*"

"Buddha, Muhammad, Allah, and other real and semimythological figures," I said, and went away from the window so fast the concussion laid all the boys out on the lawn.

I shoveled myself into ... jumper, yanked on ... and clipped my tooth-napkins to my hip-pocket, for I knew there'd be no food or even thought of food for ... we'd just stuff with pills when our stomachs barked, and fell down **the** ...

... ... all five of the boys were howling at ... lips, jumping ... I scooting.

I lost one ... and I waving them at 5000 mph, "till the Horizon is a blur ..."

On the moment, with the cylinder hissing under it to Rocket port, twenty miles from town a few miles ...

... I had there in ... ... see the sky ...

the small continental ... ... and negative ... ... this was big, among the ... ...

... ... all me in ... ...

... ... Saturday the best day in the world ...

I ... and I ... with ... ... grins. We ... ... The other pirates were okay, but ... ... now march ... around like all the ... ... and they loved the rockets, but I bet the feeling wasn't ... ... and I would do more ... ... each of us ... ... would ... ...

... ... fellows ... we laughed with the ... ... we were like a ...

in

slow motion,

it
moved

like

a

hun-
dred years of dreaming

men ran away from it

trembling

laughing

the

multitentacular

thing

stared

at me

It was

sad

* * *

dirty

flub|

funny,

lump

with   eyes

Come on inside,

I said

it

sat down

We both just sat there,
                    just sat there.

USING A HULA HOOP CAN GET YOU
ABDUCTED BY ALIENS

We've never taken anyone
buttoned up and trotting from point A
to point B—subway to office, office to
lunch, fretting over the credit crunch.
Not the ones carefully maneuvering their
whatchamacallits alongside broken white lines,
not the Leash-holders who take their Furries
to the park three point five times per day.
If you're an integer in that kind of
equation, you belong with your Far-bits
on the ground. We're seven Star-years
past calculus, so it's the dreamy ones
who want to go somewhere they don't know
how to get to that interest us, the ones
who will stare all day at a blank piece of paper
or square of canvas, then peer searchingly into
their herbal tea. It's true that hula hoops
resemble the rings around Firsthome, and that
when you spin, we chime softly, remembering
Oursummer, Ourspring and our twelve Otherseasons.
But that's not the only reason. (Do we like rhyme?
Yes we do. Also your snow, your moss, your tofu—
our sticky hands make it hard for us to put
things down.) Don't fret, dreamy spinning ones
with water falling from your faces.
It's us you're waiting for and we're coming.

CHEAP CLONING PROCESS LETS YOU HAVE YOUR OWN LITTLE ELVIS

If the real Elvis was a racecar,
the little matchbox-sized Elvi we buy
are the half-galaxies of other cars'
odometers seen through a cab window
at night. When my Elvis does a hip swivel
(like a bobblehead dog on the dash, he's game,
will swivel all day long) it doesn't cause
a full-on swoon, just a tiny pinprick
of desire felt in the arch of the foot.
Like a lozenge when you want a meal.
The Elvi are smart not to serenade us
with "Baby, If You'll Give Me All of Your Love"
on their nanoguitars—we'd crush them
with one corresponding hip spiral of our own.
They stick to strumming "Dainty Little Moonbeams"
while we smoke cigarettes and cloak them
in smoke. My friend, who's strangely loyal
to the Original Elvis timeline, maintains hers
nicely, smoothes baby oil onto his black hair.
Using a microscope, she's already sewn him
a tiny sequined jumpsuit for his later fatter years
and to that end she deep-fries breadcrumbs stuffed
with a dab of peanut butter and one Baco Bit.
Once I caught mine manhandling a sprig of parsley,
pretending it was Priscilla. Every month or so
we meet at a playground on our lunchbreak
and corral them all in a sandbox. Fights flare up
instantaneously over who's the real Elvis,
who's an impostor, and while they pull on
each other's pompadours, we munch on
our pastrami sandwiches, imagining
what's up next: a tiny Jesus, or a mini
Michael Jackson wearing Disco Barbie's glove.

PROM KING AND QUEEN SEEK
U.N. RECOGNITION OF THEIR OWN COUNTRY . . .
PROMVANIA!

Most August Council of Member Nations,
please accept this petition and attendant corsages—
roses for the ladies' wrists, magnetized magnolias
for the men's lapels. The dewdrops are glue and won't
drip. Lauren, my queen, your tiara's dents are sadly
spotlit under these fluorescents, (Sarah should
never have said that about your glorious ass), but aside
from the usual border disputes with Homecoming and
Sadie Hawkins, we're committed to peace. Pinky-swear.
Yes, of course you have questions. We know how to
spike punch to perfection and if a large percentage
of our national debt stems from the nightly balloon-falls
we require, there is much to admire in our high school
treasurer's thrift—she orders streamers in bulk and
the prom court runners-up (we'd never call them losers)
collect faux-fetti from the hole punches in the English wing.
The right to have a perfect prom is inalienable, right?
One of these nights, it's going to happen—there'll be no ex
dancing by, starry-eyed, with her strapless inching toward
topless (expect sanctions, Santana!), no need to photoshop
added sparkle onto our CVS scepters. Press your hand to your
cheek but pretend it's someone else's hand. Vote yes.

MICHELIN MAN POSSESSED
BY WILLIAM SHAKESPEARE

I've taken many forms over the years,
but this may be the strangest one. I see
through his eyes but cannot shed a tear,
I can feel his feet, but am not free
to leave this spot by the garage. I think
he feels a kind of love for the balloon
who bobs nearby. Each day he sees her sink
an inch. Though I want to tell him of the moon
and slippered feet in marble halls, these tires
at our waist are a mischief. I make believe
they are couplets of rubber, but barbed wire
would be more apt. It's very hard to breathe.
Make us a man, or make us a machine—
but do not leave us trapped here in-between.

NEPTUNE'S SETTLERS REVERT TO OLDE WORLDE WAYS

We're having lunch at the Commons
with the Critics when the message—
if you can call it that—arrives,
nine thousand days after
the settlers rocketed off for that
farthest ball in the sky. Our president
looks distinctly ill as she studies
the drawing of three children,
all unhelmeted, one with actual
Hillbetty hair sprouting on
her head. Message received.
They might as well have sent us
a Macramé manifesto. "Space madness
take four," we declare, unhappily
hitting our helmets with our hands,
tapping out *Pluto, Saturn, Mars*.
You can bet they're not pollinating
the Ultra-Tree saplings we sent them
off with, sheathed in silver mesh.
Our Sponsored Sky zippers open.
Most of the Advertisement Slinkies
make it to the stairs and start
shimmying down, but a few
bounce-glint in the plastic trees like
an ancient wingèd thing from a song.

WOMAN LIVES IN HOUSE
MADE OF PEOPLE

They were lonely. I was alone.
Out of those two sentences,

I made myself a home. My house sighs,
has a hundred heartbeats, dimpled

cupboards and a pink mouth for a mailbox.
There's always a tangle of legs in my bed.

O the walls have eyes, the baseboards
have toes. The decorative molding (rows of noses)

twitches and sniffles, and at the end
of the sad movie, the tears on my face

are not only my own. But now the outside
feels all wrong—trees not breathing,

sidewalks unspeckled by a single freckle,
and blazing over everything, a faceless sun.

ON INTIMACY

When I say we I mean
me in a wide wide dress.

MY ZEBRA SON

is still wobbly and warm
when the photogs arrive, turtle-mouthed,
their pockets bulging with lenses.
It's cheap to write stories about us
because we reproduce so well
in black & white, but the stacks
of newspapers barking ZEBRA BORN
WITH HORIZONTAL STRIPES! and ABRACADABRA,
A NEW KIND OF ZEBRA! are just a new pack
of wild dogs. The humans stare too intently
(What do they mean when they whisper
zebra tic-tac-toe, zebra gingham?), and you don't look
at all—zigzagging by, ears angry. No one
grooms him but me. When the real hyenas come,
I don't think you'll do the Congeal & Conceal
the way we usually do for our young.
I'm sorry now that I let the albino go solo
to her grave as if I didn't see the ledge.
Come closer. Give him a sniff. We're all
dominoes, dummies. Today it's him.
Tomorrow it's you, then you, then you.

MY

OCTOPUS ORPHAN

thinks his suction cups are radios.
He presses them to his head and
it's always Ma playing on AM,
Father on FM. His eyes turn inward,
and he buries himself in the sand.
When the cephalopod sonogram
comes back, it shows his poison sac is
chockablock and leaking internally,
his ink sac predictably empty after
the hundreds of gloomy telegrams
with which he's muddied the walls
of his glass world. I know it's an aquarium
cliché, but I buy him a tricked-out
shipwreck from Goldfish Utopia.
Sometimes he squashes himself inside,
leaving only his hard beak on deck
and the only way to lure him out
is with his favorite snack of snails.
He sure knows how to look lonely.
Though I hold it in the water long
enough, he never takes my hand.
He understands: there was the sea, then me.

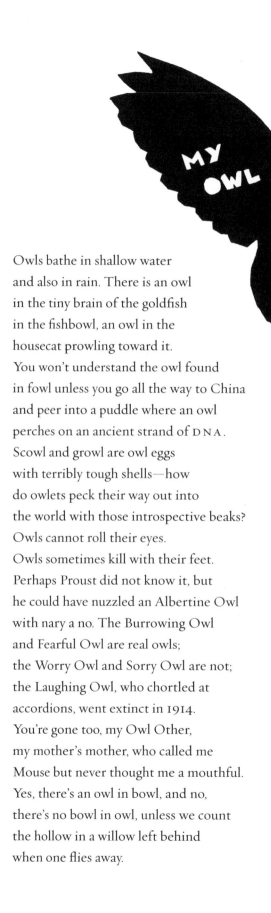

MY OWL OTHER

Owls bathe in shallow water
and also in rain. There is an owl
in the tiny brain of the goldfish
in the fishbowl, an owl in the
housecat prowling toward it.
You won't understand the owl found
in fowl unless you go all the way to China
and peer into a puddle where an owl
perches on an ancient strand of DNA.
Scowl and growl are owl eggs
with terribly tough shells—how
do owlets peck their way out into
the world with those introspective beaks?
Owls cannot roll their eyes.
Owls sometimes kill with their feet.
Perhaps Proust did not know it, but
he could have nuzzled an Albertine Owl
with nary a no. The Burrowing Owl
and Fearful Owl are real owls;
the Worry Owl and Sorry Owl are not;
the Laughing Owl, who chortled at
accordions, went extinct in 1914.
You're gone too, my Owl Other,
my mother's mother, who called me
Mouse but never thought me a mouthful.
Yes, there's an owl in bowl, and no,
there's no bowl in owl, unless we count
the hollow in a willow left behind
when one flies away.

MY WOLF SISTER

When my hole punch drizzles tiny paper circles onto the carpet, my wolf sister moans and bites it, covering her ears with her paws. I think she's tired of the moon. She takes a stack of dinner plates from my cupboard and slinks off to the park to break them. Our brother shows up a week later, collapses on the sofa like a fur throw. Why have they come here when everything I do is wrong? They howl in the shower together but the water doesn't mask the sound. I go in afterward with paper towels to mop the droplets—I know there'll be water all over—but the room is bone dry. Maybe this time things will be different. I hide the home movies in case they ask for them. In the one I always watch, there's some wobbly footage of the sky, then my father lowers the camera's eye to mother teaching my sister and brother to "tell time." They're following a mother hare on her sunset rounds—one leveret mouthful at 12 o'clock, another at 3, 6 and 9. Then the camera zooms in on me—I've spat out my pacifier made of fur and I'm on the porch surrounded by bonsai trees, killing or saving Barbie.

MY BIRD FAMILY

was spooling out a mournful song, *A misbegotten*
gulp in the gizzard, ice on the clenched claw after
a blizzard, when I swooped in with my solo:
a bird filled with lead is better off dead.
For a change, we weren't larking about
in our strap-on beaks. I had been a finch filled
with certainty until the end of the talk
about the universe at which point I was just
a diminutive coo lost in the bamboo, an "or"
in a grove I thought was mine. The others too.
We fell backward into dreaming.
Somewhere was a park bench covered in
down, or a complicated carousel of up,
hatching new angles of flight which would outnumber
every plane contrail, every kite hypotenuse,
every lip-licking catleap toward the birdhouse.
In the sandpit we collided with toddler-made
castles and were none the worse, though the sky
spun slightly. The clouds turned back to meringue.
Sometimes we stretched out a courageous claw
and climbed back into our cages, just to see
the human look in at us with his giant eyes,
to let his booming whistle swish through our feathers.

The world is already crowded with instructions—crosswalks, implications, clues. We've projected too much on the moon. Maybe that's why they switched to stars? The No More Suicide Fox constellation looks astonishingly unadmonishing. His face is sweet and a little sad, as if he was copied from some coloring book from the fifties. Maybe he helps the happy ones go to sleep in their happy beds, no longer needing to make their sad ones promise "I won't, I won't." The children chant, "Star light, star bright, no one dies tonight," but I'm not convinced. Where is he during the days, the gray days or the ones too bright with sunlight? We need a dog patrol that sniffs out despair and a horde of someones who will ask every single person every single day, "Are you okay?" before another friend is found dead in the bathtub, on the floor. I don't want to talk about that fox. He's pointing at people I know.

The new constellations are spelled out—as if someone has decided we're too dumb to make up new myths and took a didactic pin to our Tyvek sky. These ones have whiskers, eyes, and stories embedded in their very names, which appear in the papers the day after their first sighting. Replacing Cassiopeia, the Retaliation Rat—one foot off the floor and headed to your door. Babies point and say *rattattatat*. The older children intuitively dislike it—it requires no rigmarole of tents and telescopes, no pointing parent, no connect-the dots— and would like it less if they knew what it will mean to them specifically: one severed dollhead = one violin left out in the rain. Hit me once and I'll hit you again. Does it ease the pain of the survivor hiding in a tree as gunshots ring out and her village turns hazy with flame? If so, it's because she hopes the rat is made of cameras not fabricated stars, and that fifty lenses are recording each last atrocity, beaming the images to some central judgment room. There always have been and always will be rooms like this, but no one in them is watching anyone that far away. They're busy. A bomb has landed and a bomb needs to be launched right back.

THE RADIO ANIMALS

The radio animals travel in lavender clouds. They are always chattering, they are always cold. Look directly at the buzzing blur and you'll see twitter, hear flicker—that's how much they ignore the roadblocks. They're rabid with doubt. When a strong sunbeam hits the cloud, the heat in their bones lends them a temporary gravity and they sink to the ground. Their little thudding footsteps sound like "Testing, testing, 1 2 3" from a faraway galaxy. Like pitter and its petite echo, patter. On land, they scatter into gutters and alleyways, pressing their noses into open Coke cans, transmitting their secrets to the silver circle at the bottom of the can. Of course, we've wired their confessionals and hired a translator. We know that when they call us Walkie Talkies they mean it scornfully, that they disdain our in- and outboxes, our tests of true or false.

THE MORAL ANIMALS

The moral animals were practicing near the stables again, inching between the slats of the horse jumps, crawling around on their hands and knees. Their leader slammed her head into a bucket of water, just frozen, and emerged bright-cheeked, blood trickling from her forehead and pooling above one eyebrow. She looked righteous. Though they would never admit it, some of them still fantasized about policemen and turnstiles, the weight of the silver bar against your stomach, the delicious click as it lets you through. Sitting on their heels in rows, the moral animals studied the blurry boundary of the sunset until it disappeared. Then it was back to mowing the fields of flowers so the sightlines were clear, chanting, *Diplomacy is a plume in the hat, what we need is war.*

INSIDE
THE
GLASS
FACTORY

The girls bend over conveyor belts, lean
into kilns, bobbing like birds diving for fish.
One taps a finished porthole window
with a small silver hammer and
pronounces it sound (outside
a woodpecker smashes its beak
into a white birch, searching for sap).
One girl runs her finger down the seam
of a serving plate (outside floodwater
makes a mirror of the meadow).
Another girl holds a thermometer
up to the light (the sun has inched up
a few degrees and yes, Monday has a fever).
Another dips her finger into
a beaker of water and tests
that each goblet in the set sings
a successive note in an E minor scale—
six notes the other girls know so well
that at night, in the dormitory,
one or all of them can be heard
hum-dreaming the song in their sleep.

Since they're not allowed outside—
never have been, never will be—
they used to watch rainstorms
like television, cross-legged, wiping
the glass if their breath fogged
the view. They used to exclaim
over drops of dew. They used to
run their fingers along the walls,
searching for a way out, but that only
smeared the sky. At break they lie
on their stomachs in the sunroom,
where they've stacked a wall of cracked
glass hands. Looking through it is the closest
they come to touching the things they see—
the horizon a lifeline across one palm,
the pine trees in the distance like
bonsai in tiny finger terrariums.
Moving things—foxes and half-moons—
slink in and out of adjacent wrists,
slide under successive glass fingernails.
Once a stag walked past and scraped
its antlers along the glass wall.
They all gasped. It was the closest
they had ever come to another body.

Now as if their skull walls had
windows and each brain were
a clear, crystalline thing, the synapses
making temporary chandeliers
of thought-sparks in the brain's
blank sky, they are all having
the same idea at the same time—
to make a girl out of glass.
The sketches start out simple, but soon
one girl proposes a glass voicebox
strung with glass chimes, another petitions
for porthole pupils, a fringe of glass
lashes on each eyelid's hinge, another
imagines a mouth made of powdered
glass and crinkled enamel, and off they go.
Not one finger here has ever felt fur,
seen veins or bones except under
the cover of skin, but they bypass
all that with the force of their dreaming—
how best to make her glass hair seem to
stream down her back, whose forefinger
they should choose to dent in her dimples.

The thermometer hits one thousand
degrees and suddenly she's standing there—
hot, glowing, almost still liquid. Like them,
but unlike too. They don't question that
she is alive, walking, gesturing. But no one
imagined that she, with her new glass eyes
would be able to see the glass lock
and the glass key. In an instant, she opens
the door and they stream outside into
the solid world. This isn't at all what
they imagined. The sky is like lead
above their heads. The once-silent birds
flood their ears with clashing arias.
All the puddles on the path are blurred
with mud. The glass girl disappears
and they don't go after her. When they finally
reach the forest—it is miles farther
than they imagined—the air inside is hazy
with dust and spores. They can't see much
beyond their fingers. A bear or maybe
a deer thuds by. When they come upon
a stream, for a moment they brighten:
the light prances on its surface like the prisms
they make in the factory, but they can't
see through to the fish, or the shadows
of fish flitting along the river floor.

Weeks later, they are back in the factory,
busily pouring bright liquids from
one beaker to another, sliding barefoot
between kiln, conveyor belt, workshop.
Then sleep. In her dreams, the girl who
has begun building a glass owl
from the inside-out, starting with
its morning meal of mouse, will invent
a formula for flight. Another is designing
a glass ladder where each rung has
a different horizon hidden inside.
The glass girl could be anywhere.
She could be just outside, watching
or she could be worlds away, and truly,
they like it that way. In the hot afternoon,
the girls melt into various poses by
the glass walls, molding their memories
of the outside world into newer, clearer forms.
One taps a finished porthole window
with a small silver hammer and pronounces it
sound. One runs her finger down the seam
of a serving plate. Another holds a thermometer
horizontally, and uses its markings to measure
the height of the trees. The mercury inside
shivers in the newly imagined breeze.

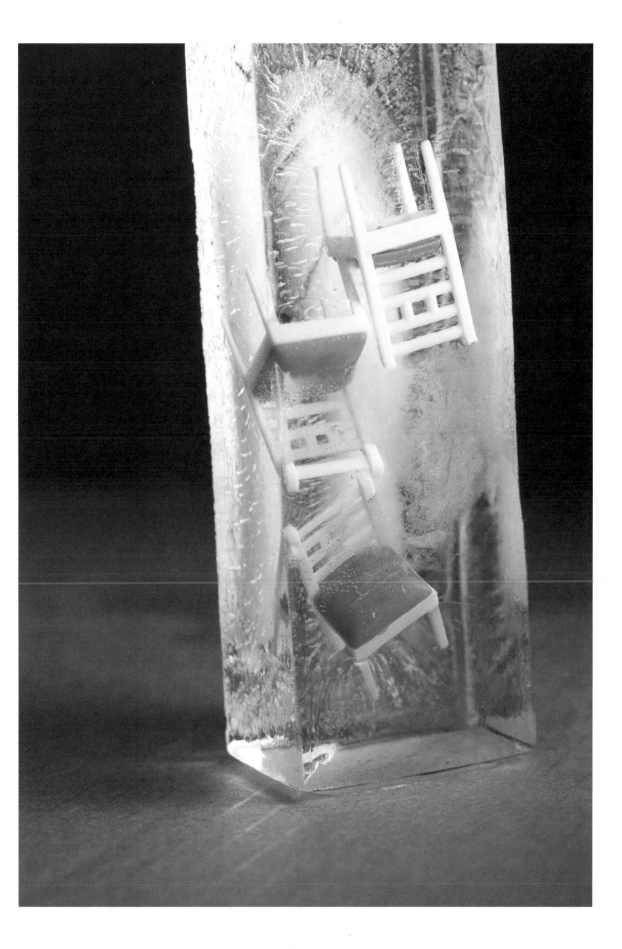

WHEN THE WATER IS AT OUR ANKLES

Unwedge the ruler you use to prop up your
window and meet me in the street. I'll bring
the measuring tape curled in the desk drawer
like a sullen snail, and hand in hand, we'll watch
as the water creeps up an inch, then two.
The river's a baby, it's a toddler, it's grown.
The lecture series never made it past Puddles.
When the water is at our knees, will someone
please pick a plan? Plan A: A fleet of sunken
subway-car reefs where fish with oil-clogged gills
can find some relief hovering in the newly calm water,
as eels coil around silver poles still smeared with
commuters' coughs and fingerprints. When the water
is at our waists, Plan B: Let loose the artificial islands,
one squirrel per. Also, the giant lilypads and the piles
of ash some of us have been saving for this occasion.
When the water is at our shoulders, the officials will
roll out the boulders and we'll throw our bonsais in
the river to simulate that underground forest they said
might help—a miniature, misplaced effort, it's true.
Our codicil to Plan C's a bust. Years of scrupulous snipping
(my bristly little juniper, your tiny sugar maple) sink
with nary a bubble or clank of ceramic pot hitting rock.
Someone's child goes bobbing by in a flotation device
made of empty milk jugs and waterwings. A dog, no two,
go under. Now, as the last bit of ice melts and the water
laps at the balconies, it's too late for Plans D through Z:
the oyster extravaganza, the lobster boats piled with biscuits,
all those dear dioramas with their rescue dramas and
baby-blue waves the size of a doll's hand, that approach
                    but never reach our once-dry land.

THERE'S A STRING ATTACHED TO EVERYTHING

The puppet snob is born by being dropped from above. And so, she's found there, in a field of daffodils, lifted up by a pair of arms and that lifting defines her. Does she love puppets from the very beginning? Yes she does. Was she a snob from the start? Hard to say. As a little girl, she remembers gluing pebbles to the hooves of her horse marionette so it could properly clomp across the stage. After her birthday cake candles are blown out for her, year after year, she watches them exit stage right, longing to be allowed to study their new melted poses. She learns to endure the Meanwhile Music in elevators as she's lifted to a different floor, but finger puppets make her scream—a woolen crowd with no nuance of motion? Hideous. As a teenager, the puppet snob restricts herself to the study of the proscenium of her beloved's forehead. The unpredictable curtains of his hair announce "end of show" at the strangest of times. Then one day, time turns artificial—perforated at the edges of her waking and sleeping—so each day can be ripped out like stage directions. There's no free will in the way the puppet snob puts her head in her hands and cries (sob, sob, twitch of the strings), no free will in the toddler, stubbornly planted on the sidewalk, toes pointed inward. Better to watch kites in the park with their unabashedly visible tethers. Better to join the charade—superglue an invisible thread to a dollar bill and wait. Is there a God? Probably not. A puppeteer, maybe.

ONE WAY

Where the first one came from,
we'll never know, but once it landed,
it did what arrows do—it pointed.
The headlines read NEW SHAPE DISCOVERED:
ARROW INVENTS THE STRAIGHT AND NARROW.
Children who had been content to trail
snails around the patio suddenly made
a gesture we'd never seen before—
holding one arm out in front of their chests
then curling in all but the longest finger.
They wanted to go to the playground
and slide down the slide with determined
smiles. They pointed at the girl with a blotch
of tomato soup on her shirt, the ape with alopecia,
and laughed with an unfriendly new note
in their laughter. Arrows led to purchases.
Arrows led to adieus. A simple shape
had turned us all from cars into ambulances,
keening with intent. The weatherman no longer
ambled aimlessly around our TV screen.
When he pointed at Chicago then Boston,
the people sitting on sofas in those cities
suddenly felt how very different from one another
they were. Dogs pulled at their leashes,
sparrows vectored through trees, knitters turned
to welding. Though there was no denying that
the "this way up" signs on parcels meant that
more vases arrived at their destinations intact,
the new words that mushroomed into being
were problematic—initiative, tomorrow, your fault,
mine. Couples sat in restaurants launching them
back and forth over the bread basket.
Soon we'd invent bows, cannons, guns.

LAST STOP DREAMLAND

The Treatzcart rattles down the train
corridor, hoovering up potato chip packets,
crumpled napkins like so many squashed
sailboats, half-eaten muffins rolling south
toward baggage. Its wheels may need oiling,
no, do need oiling, but its heart—the vermilion
thermos of coffee stowed in its very center—
is strong as a song. The Treatzcart is careful about feet,
so careful about feet. Once someone slapped
it, and the cart thought, "This will serve me a lesson
to look where I step," and in a parallel world,
the Tin Man was pleased. Through the window,
a flash of a horse nodding in the field (nose to
the hay, nose to the sky) and the chorus
of sugar maples above singing almost there, nary
a care, as the passengers gather their reflections
from the windows and slap them back onto
their faces and chests, flex their feet, and
arch their backs to erase the shape of their sitting.
The ice cubes are all melted, the books are
stowed away, and as people exit the train,
they look dazed, hazier, as if their bits aren't
quite put back together. The Treatzcart hums
along happily—soon it will start over, chugging
down the aisles offering bagels, coffee, juice.
It loves to watch the faces waver as they choose.

QUICK MAKE A MOAT

Before the rain, only baseballs
and baby birds fell from the sky.
We had Puddles-from-Below
made by sprinklers or toddler
go-getters with spoons,
but the Puddles-from-Above
were unpredictable, indiscriminate.
They made mud where we hadn't
planned for mud. They made us
complain. Our succulent gardens
rotted at the roots and caved in.
Trees—formerly so rare, so cherished—
took their places and we soon took
to cutting them down. Naturally,
fountains fell out of favor. The umbrellas—
marvelous and necessary inventions
though they were—made us private,
prone to secrets. No matter how large
they were or how high we held them,
they never seemed to shelter more than
one. Twos dwindled in every arena—
doubles tennis, duets, tangos. Why bother
to hold hands? We'd been singled out
by the rain for other things. The storm
clouds racing across the formerly blank sky
narrowed our options. Gone the sun
and its dance partner the moon.
Tucked in our twin beds, pushed as far
apart as possible, we listen to the gutters'
angry gush and try to dream our way back
to the time before rain, when we never
woke to find the car in the driveway
suddenly effortlessly sparkling clean.

GAME FOR ANYTHING

A plane-shaped silence flies
overhead. "Thought that up,"

thinks the Phenom, doing
arm-circles in the bright arena

between sun and moon. Poor Every-
girl, at first the air is everywhere

she runs. Hers isn't the face
stenciled on our socks.

She knows the gods don't care
where the ball goes.

When the reflector makes
the ball-bird double

back, the Phenom goes wild
in the shadows of the umpire chair,

but it's a no-go in the slo-mo.
In the setting sun, our binoculars

are ten thousand flaming hoops.
I start a cheer. I get everyone saying it

like they've been saying it for years.

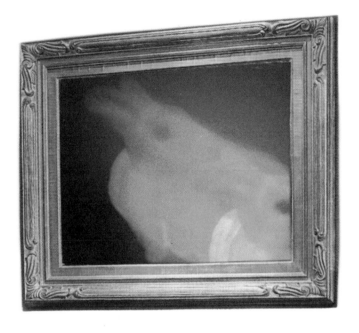

The sun was dim then done, but after months of treatments, the animals did begin to glow. Elephants tried to siphon the light from their bellies, trunkful by glowing trunkful. Rabbits tried to outwit it, leaping up, then sideways, ears pressed back like china rabbits, eyes all eyelid but for one dark slit. During the Age of Failed Cures we didn't go outside for fear of seeing lemurs crunching on light switches, rats swaddling themselves in the thick gray blankets movers use, dogs digging holes for the others to die in. Then they began to run. A bright shrieking blur screamed down side streets and highways as if it would never stop. On the eighth day it did. The animals came back into focus and though their eyes were different, otherwise they acted the same as before—eating, sleeping, nipping at their fur. At the ski resort, a man makes snow by the glow of one hibernating bear. In the malls, lit sparrows flit along, guiding the shoppers' way. Before we undress, as usual, we shoo the dog from the bedroom. In our heads we can still see the moon.

In the fever hospital, the elevator
moves like a bead of mercury
between floors. The higher the floor
the higher the fever—down here
we're allowed cards but the bouquets
are whisked up and away to where
the peonies' pinks pinch their way
into already-blooming cheeks, roses'
reds flood the invalids' flushed faces.
Down here, only black and white movies
and then they're always about deserts.
They want us burning. There's no
pushing of ice chips past our purple lips.
We're squeezed into tight silk pajamas
under more wool blankets than can possibly
be necessary, our heads on velvet pillows

so they can get an imprint of our sweat.
If it forms the outline of an animal,
an orderly scuttles down the hall, keening.
They wear only the most practical shoes.
Their pockets bulge with syringes.
We know that if we're "promoted"
the nightmares will only get worse,
but we yearn for a top-floor view,
just one bit of blue, a chance to see
the clothesline flagged with handkerchiefs
as a clothesline and nothing more, before
the hallucinations begin, before the clothesline
morphs into a giant gap-toothed grin
and the mirage-milkers tiptoe in.

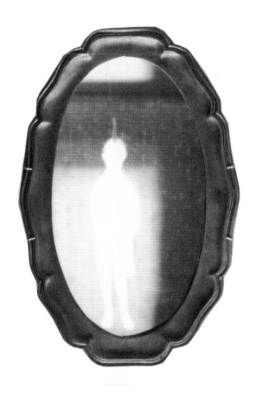

The stereotypes stand on streetcorners mostly, never in their neighborhood of origin where their hair might be too shiny, their face too flat—there you'd see how wrong they are, drawn with a Sharpie, not a 0.5 mm pen. They thrive in places where they are different, where people believe in that difference—the one tree shedding its coppery leaves on a street full of spring. You have to see them from a certain angle to sense they aren't real, or overhear the tired strings of clichés they mutter as they bend over to tie a shoelace. When on the move, they glide along invisible streetcar grooves, making perfect right-angle turns. On this morning of prettiest sunshine, there is one hovering near my bus stop, gobbling up the specificities of the group on the bench. There's the businessman folding the days's headlines neatly into his briefcase underneath a bit of Stilton, a curvy girl with Giselle stiched in cursive on her backpack, and me. With my love of poetry, fear of rashes and mixed feelings about zoos, I like to think I'm a Christmas tree tricked out in similes, not one store-bought thought hanging on me, but if I sniff a peony, is it a pose? Do I smile generally and at no one in particular?

Because twilight is a triplet,
today we're beginning with C,
and the puzzle is of a creek

that freezes and unfreezes as you go.
When the puzzle piece slots in,
it's like ziplock, ad hoc Matlock.

This is not the FYI convention,
but I'll tell you about my inventions:
hors d'oeuvres served the next day

as jour d'après, flesh spackle for the cleft
of chin, my patented way to admit adultery:
Let Your Wife Know with Footsteps in Snow.

Shall we count ourselves lucky? 1.2.3.

On Rhyme's first day at school, the teacher, Ms. P, doesn't write his name on the board or introduce him to the class, and for that, he's grateful. But though he holds both hands up when she asks a question, she never calls on him. Soon he's making spitballs out of the haiku handout and shooting them two at a time at Fragment, an ethereal girl with a choppy haircut who answers, "Five . . . or nineteen . . . or . . ." She trails off. She's the star pupil, sits in the head of the class, her feet (one shod in a shoe, the other bare) crossed at her ankles. It rankles. Shunned at recess by the Sestina twins who are playing an elaborately modified version of badminton, with marks in the sand where each shot has to be hit from, Rhyme slinks inside and secretly arranges the children's raincoats in an ABAB CDCD EFEF color pattern, then buttons or zips them up. The purple coat has no pair so he stuffs it in the trash, next to which sit the teacher's green rain boots—GG. Once his heart has regained its regular beat, he spends a few glorious minutes going up and down the long silver slide, not yet hot with the newly shining sun. It's fun, but lunch is another story. Fragment is eating a cherry tomato with one chopstick. Free Verse sits down next to Rhyme and opens up his sandwich to reveal a mushroom-colored, nasty looking, pungent paste. "Goose pâté," he whispers significantly, "made from Mother Goose." For the rest of the day, Rhyme keeps his head low over his desk, funneling his tears into his plastic orange pencil sharpener. By the last bell, it's full. As the line of children files out, he looks hopefully at the gate latch, but he's shoved to the middle of the line, and Ms. P leaves the gate swinging open.

Our American husbands were born
on a day of cartoon clouds and neon sun.
They don't remember their fathers
whispering Ferris wheel lullabies over
their cradles, but they can do somersaults
while smoking. Their banter is full of data.
They have kiss quotas and the shoulders
of soldiers. While our small selves made
toast points and played post office,
they were practicing love-hate with
the heads of state. I've asked, so I know
our American husbands didn't have hamsters;
they had can-do cats and piggy banks.
Don't get me wrong—I've added
up my toys a time or two, but when
they whistle dixie, I wonder.
Remember the Halloween I was a Bruise
and you were a Moving Picture
and our American husbands picked masks
that made the most of their noses? Sister,
I envy that with the zippers on their jackets
they can mimic the sound of rain.
When our American husbands take out
the trash, the garbage-engorged flies
don't thud against their heads.
They have extravagant smiles
and can run for miles. When they go
into their studies, they study.

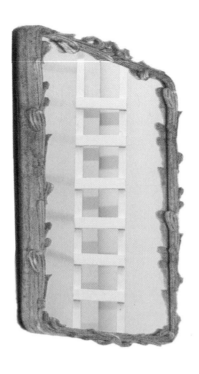

In the hell between heavens of nothingness, we, with once-wet cloths stuck to our foreheads, our watches strapped the wrong way onto our wrists, are finally being given a chance. This morning, there were signs: a nurse knocked over a jar filled with bendy straws and didn't pick them up. Breakfast in its five sectionals, each one less appetizing than the next, never arrived. An hour ago they came in and unplugged all the HELP buttons, folded the bed railings underneath the mattresses like unnecessary wings and unlocked the brakes on our wheelchairs. We heard the elevator door open—ding—and close— ding. A few of us can still speak and when someone gasped out, "treasure hunt" you could tell from the way the drooping heads stiffened that they had heard the rumors too. We, who have not had control over the curtains for as long as we can remember, immediately get to it—rooting through flowerpots, frisking the file folders for directions or clues, but there's no sign of that pistol anywhere. Through our smeared glasses we watch our urine bags grow fuller and darker than ever before. No one finds the gun, but we make what tiny attacks we can. I hit Sally on the head with some wilted flowers, she squeezes my bag of saline as hard as she can, but she's too weak to make it pop. We do this out of love.

No-Hands has hands but he keeps them clenched in fists at his chest. He appeared long ago on the dustiest day. Some say the sunset sent him. The children are fearless—they'll caress the two moles on the back of his right hand, bring their softest animals to rub past his bare ankles. When the town comittee put the most delicious cake (with glossy fondant and candied pansies) in front of No-Hands, he didn't lunge for it, didn't even lick his lips. No one has seen him eat, but we imagine him gnawing on the fruit of low-hanging branches, licking the leftover jello from the schoolchildren's lunch trays. If we could discover his diet, we'd remake his food with twice the butter and cream, sit back and wait until his ballooning belly forced his arms out and away from his body. We're not thinking "ta-da!"—flock of doves or drawbridge comma princess, but we do dream about his fingers unfurling like sea anemones. We just want him to understand the hose dribbling next to each tree, why I give you something and you take it from me.

This is what the Last Ones left us.
After the Era of Flood and after the Era
of Fire, we creep into the Central Clusters
and rifle through the rubble. From the top
of a cliff, two pink eyes and one pale ear beckon.
The Wordsplitter names the creature
Kangamouse, Male. It is not one of their BeWiths,
which were almost universally furred,
nor a ListenTo, since he makes no sound,
nor is there a mention of Kangamouse
in the *Aesop's Fables* found in a Ziploc
in Zone Twelve some twenty years ago.
We still cannot make a Ziploc, but we know
all about Morals—try before you trust and
might makes right. We try to tease one out.
If a "mouse" can make its home in a hole, are we
to understand we will live on without the sun?
If the "kangaroo" keeps its children in a pocket,
is it wise to keep our Gimmes close too though
they wail and steal our food? Perhaps Kangamouse
has something to do with their mysterious notion of "Play"—
a type of waiting for sunset that involved throwing
spheres and grimacing. He may well be yet another
Withholder, since when we press on his button,
like all the other Gods we've found and abandoned,
nothing happens. "Night makes light," we murmur, and look
up at the sky with the face the Last Ones called Hope.

TELETTROFONO

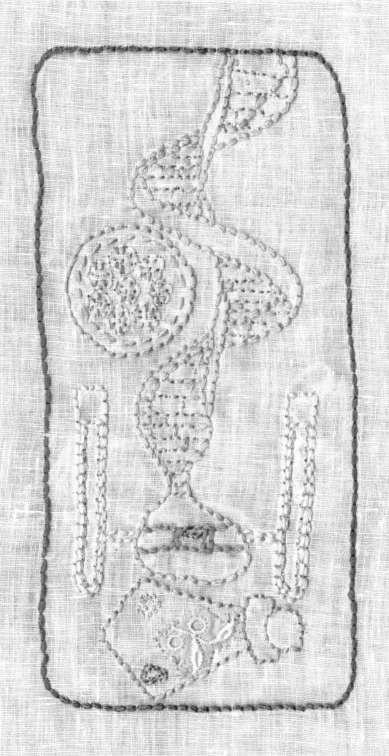

Fig. 1 TELETTROFONO CROSS-SECTION

PRESET INSTRUCTION MODE

Hello? Please turn off all twenty-first-century gadgets, as they will interfere with the delicate instrument you are holding in your hand.

PRESET ANTONIO MEUCCI MONOLOGUE MODE

It looks plastic and unbeautiful, no? But oh if you filleted this telettrofono, the wonders you would see. Two tubes lined with fish scales and mercury, sparks of electricity tripping up tiny gold stairs, a spirit level stitched into a swimbladder, a microphone made of minimolluscs, and, floating in a small stoppered vial, one petticoat snippet, one mermaid tear, and a cell from the gill of an electric eel. You are holding in your hand "the telephone which I invented and which I first made known and which, as you know, was stolen from me." (FIG. 1)

PRESET VERIFIABLE FACT MODE

Whereas inventor Antonio Meucci is born in 1808 in Florence, Italy. Whereas in 1833 he begins work as a stagehand at the Teatro della Pergola where he meets his future wife, Esterre Mochi, born 1815, a seamstress who is rumored to have been a mermaid. Whereas all primary sources for the previous intimation have gone missing, but murmurs persist in the sounds of the sea, and what is the sea if not primary?

PRESET STAGE DIRECTION MODE

Listen for the audience settling into their seats—coughs bouncing between balconies, ladies tucking their toes under their petticoats, low murmurs between lovers, handkerchiefs shaken out and folded back into pockets, the hushed voices of ushers, violinists plucking strings, twisting their tuning pegs . . . As the sound decrescendos (you'll know it when it happens)—*now*—let the first backdrop fall, then slowly pull on the cord that raises the curtain.

PRESET MERMAID MONOLOGUE MODE (ESTERRE MEUCCI)

Look up. The clouds are a pod of belugas,
the sun, a bloom of jellyfish fluorescing
a few fathoms up, or no, make it nighttime—
the light underwater was never this bright.
That was once my life. I moved through it
smoothly, too smoothly—sometimes just to feel
something, I'd take—between my thumb
and forefinger—one of the many hooks
that were hunting underwater and give it a tug.
Hello, I mouthed underwater, *hello?*

PRESET VERIFIABLE FACT MODE

The name Esterre means "star." Antonio means "worthy of praise."

PRESET FAIRY TALE MODE

Once upon a time in the time.
of once upon a time, there was

a mermaid who longed for sound—
not for whale songs moodily bumping
for miles along the ocean floor or
the soft swish of tiny fish gills pulsing
in and out, but for what she heard
when her ears broke through the
water's surface. Crack of thunder.
Waves walloping the rocks.

PRESET PATENT MODE

PATENT 122477 IMPROVEMENTS IN LONG-DISTANCE LISTENING
(IMAGINED)

(Esterre wants her ears closer to the clouds,
wants them to stretch over the water
so she can hear the opposite shore.
You give her one thing, she wants more.
I bring her a hare after a long day of hunting
and she cries and strokes its long ears.)

PRESET MERMAID MONOLOGUE MODE (ESTERRE MEUCCI)

Humans, let me tell you something. Mermaids,
sirens, shipwreckers, whatever you call us
on a particular day, we don't abandon the sea
for love or legs—we fling ourselves onto the shore
for *sound*. I mooned around for years waiting for
the carp's accordion gills to wheeze out a tune, for
a deafening chorus from those wide-mouthed anemones.
Monday was muffled. Tuesday mute, until Sunday
I smashed my head through the barrier between sea
and sky and there was the two-ton wave-timpani,
the puffin's claws click-click-clicking as it skidded
to a stop on the cliff's edge, rain spanking the sea
until it wailed. I clapped my hands and the claps
echoed back like an answer. Yes. Yes. Yes. Yes.
Between the third and fourth yes, my tail split
in two, sprouted knees and feet, toes.

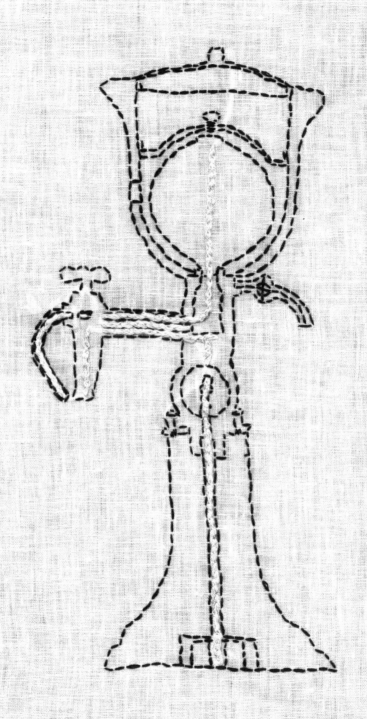

No. 122478 EFFERVESCENT DRINKS

PRESET PATENT MODE

PATENT 122478 IMPROVEMENT IN THE MANUFACTURE
OF EFFERVESCENT DRINKS FROM FRUITS (APPROVED)

Esterre: Louder please.

Antonio: How's this?

Esterre: Still not loud enough.

Esterre: Can you make it louder?

(Esterre is disappointed that the fizz isn't louder.)

PRESET MATH PROBLEM MODE

A mermaid swims from the Mediterranean into the Ligurian Sea and up the
Arno River. She climbs onto the riverbank at 7:02 p.m. and, drawn by a far-
off aria, makes her way to an opera house 1.7 kilometers away at an average
rate of four kilometers per hour (accounting for her wobbly new legs).
Starting at 6 p.m. and ending at 12 p.m., a stagehand climbs up and down the
theater scaffolding twelve times, averaging a distance of twenty meters on
each journey at an average rate of five kilometers per hour, and goes down the
backstage stairs (an extra twelve meters) at 7:30 p.m., 8:50 p.m. and 9:40 p.m.
Will the mermaid and the stagehand meet on the stairs? If so, what distance
will they each have traveled and what time will it be? If the opera begins at
8 p.m. and the stage notes call for thunder at 8:20 p.m., rain at 8:22 p.m., and
lightning at 10:12 p.m., what sound, if any, will be in the background when the
mermaid and the stagehand meet?

PRESET INSTRUCTION MODE

If you find one, pick up a shell. See if it purrs when you scratch it.

PRESET ANTONIO MEUCCI MONOLOGUE MODE

I heard her before I saw her—the costumes
she designed were all about sound—
the whisper-swish-catch of gauze against
raw satin, corsets ringed with tiny bells,
shoes with metal plates on the toes and suede
on the heels, clack-shuffling across the stage.
She must have seen me listening, because
a few nights later, when I put my ear to

the speaking tube I'd made for the director
to talk to the stagehands perched in the trellises,
there was only one word waiting, *Meucci*, *Meucci*,
over and over, as if she were calling for
a pet cat, followed by a giggle that sounded
like water running down steps of glass.

PRESET MARINE TELEPHONE MODE (MERMAID CHORUS)
Once, a large square mammal with a wide mouth
of black and white teeth floated up out of a shipwreck.
It's true, we swam away. We'd never seen a piano before.

PRESET PATENT MODE
PATENT 122479 WAVE METRONOME (IMAGINED)

PRESET MAIN TELETTROFONO MODE
Hello, Antonio? Last night
I dreamt that giant white
mountains came crashing
down on me.

PRESET VERIFIABLE FACT MODE
When she lived in Staten Island, Esterre had a cat called Lillina who had
a total of twenty-four kittens and then those kittens had kittens.... Their
descendants are everywhere.

PRESET PATENT MODE
PATENT 122480 GIANT STONE PIANO (IMAGINED)
(I spent a whole night lugging the stone keys
into place, but when the whole octave
was there on the sand and I tried to play it—
hitting the keys with rocks and bits
of driftwood—it wasn't at all as I'd imagined.
No thunder. No music of the gods. Instead,
a sad little thud sonata. A dud étude. Go ahead.
Try it out. Esterre didn't like it either.)

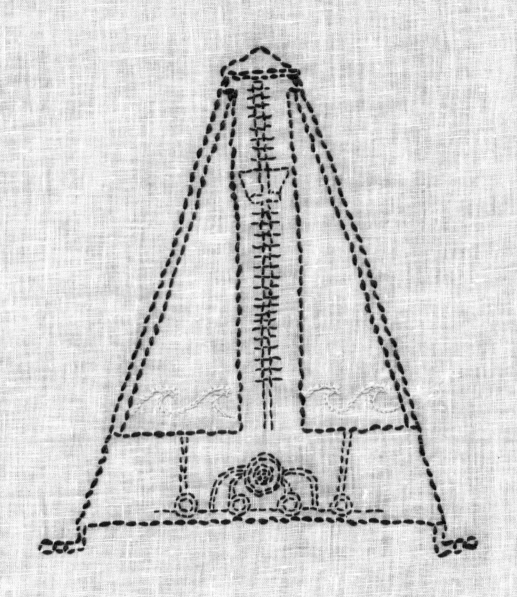

No. 122479 WAVE METRONOME

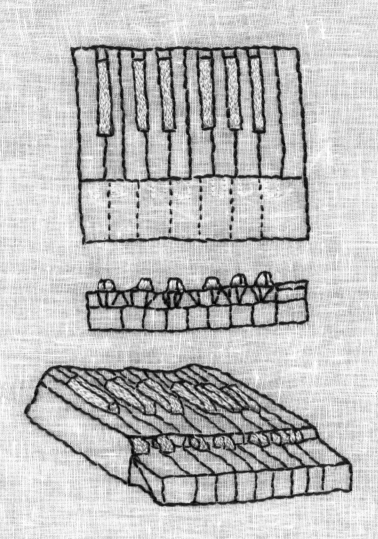

No. 122480 GIANT STONE PIANO

PRESET INSTRUCTION MODE
Keep your eyes open for mermaids.

PRESET ANTONIO MEUCCI MONOLOGUE MODE
Her sharpest, brightest needle—her *piccolo delfino*
or little dolphin—was always diving in and out
of the seas of fabric on her lap. Weeks later
she'd show me the curse stitched inside the belt
of the cranky tenor that made him crack on his high
C. At the time, my magic was minimal—turn the
crank and watch the cardboard waves roll, pound
the sheet of metal for thunder.... She gave me scraps
of white cotton and muslin for my snow cradle—
we suspended the bag above the stage and a man
in each wing shook the strings gently, gently
so the snow-cloth sifted through the holes
in the bag and drifted down onto the singers.
That snow scene was the only silent thing that
ever made her smile. The lights worked wonders
though—the night I brought her onto the stage and lit
the candles, each with a mirror angled behind it
and a sheet of blue glass in front, she stamped
her new feet with delight and said, "Daylight!"

PRESET VERIFIABLE FACT MODE
Esterre never learned to read
or write. She signed documents
with an *x*, like a cross-stitch.

PRESET MARINE TELEPHONE MODE (MERMAID CHORUS)
Your human's brain sounds like
an octopus. He needs a fin to guide him.

PRESET VERIFIABLE FACT MODE

Whereas Antonio Meucci and Esterre Mochi marry on August 7, 1834, at the church of Santa Maria Novella, Florence. Whereas in 1835, Esterre and Antonio sail to Havana (with seventy-nine other members of the Italian Opera Company and thirty-five tons of props and equipment) to work at the Gran Teatro Tacón, a new Cuban opera house. Whereas Antonio is appointed superintendent of mechanism, Esterre head of the tailoring department. Whereas Antonio devises a water-filtering system for Havana, diverts a river under the opera house to improve its acoustics, and is commissioned to set up an electroplating factory by the Cuban army. Whereas Antonio, while experimenting with electric shock therapy, discovers that electricity can allow sound to travel along a wire. Whereas one of the operas performed in the Gran Teatro Tacón is *Ernani* by Verdi. Act One begins in the mountains of Aragon.

PRESET PATENT MODE

PATENT 183062 IMPROVEMENT IN HYGROMETERS, FOR MEASURING HUMIDITY (APPROVED)

"I prefer for general use to give all the parts an ornamental appearance, imitating the person of a weather-prophet or some other significant device."
(Esterre thought it should have been a mermaid and stitched a revision onto my handkerchief. She did recommend the whalebone after all.)

PRESET ANTONIO MEUCCI MONOLOGUE MODE

The mountains are crumbling in the ship's hold.
There's no mold—from my experiments
I knew enough to remind the scene painters
to mix clove oil into the papier-mâché—but sea air
is stringent stuff and though we wedged
the mountains between trunks and packed
their peaks with blankets, when the waves
toss our ship like a toy and forks go flying

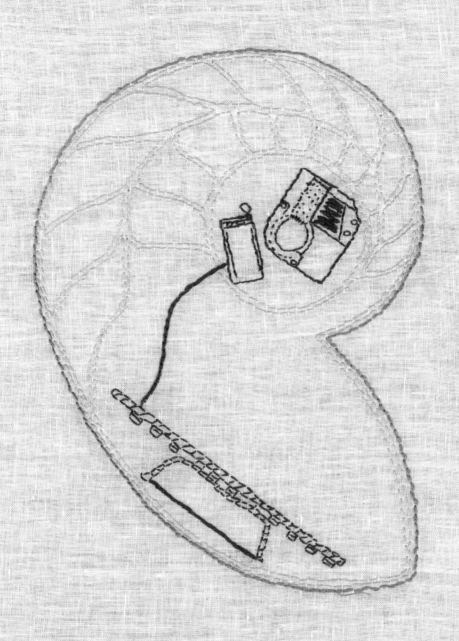

No. 125444 PURRING SHELL

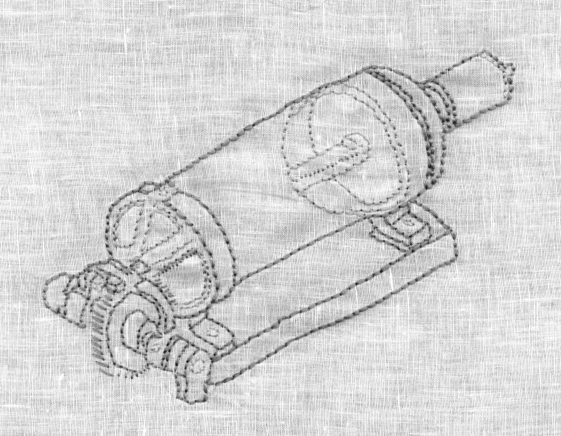

No. 122970 FOG APPARATUS

in the mess hall, I can feel the fissures
forming. Aneto, the largest mountain,
has already cracked in two, and bits of it
are sifting like salt into the floorboards.
All the carefully painted shadows and ridges,
the line of firs, even the tiny path (a folly,
since you couldn't see it from the first row)
have peeled off. Just yesterday, Esterre found
a mountain hut stuck to the heel of my shoe.

PRESET STAGE DIRECTION MODE

For the best tempest, attach a drum or drums to a roll of canvas. If you do
not have an electrostatic lightning machine (truly, these are the best, though
they can malfunction in humid weather), cut two pieces of wood with forked
edges so that when they are fit together, no light can get through. Place these
in front of a very bright chandelier. When it is time for lightning, separate
and close. Repeat.

PRESET PATENT MODE

PATENT 122970 DEVICE FOR INDICATING THE POSITION OF
SHIPS IN FOG (PATENT NEVER FILED)

PRESET PATENT MODE

PATENT 122973 BLEACHING PROCESS TO TURN RED CORAL PINK
(PATENT NEVER FILED)
(Esterre prefers the pink. Some men
will do anything for their wives, I think.)

PRESET VERIFIABLE FACT MODE (ANTONIO MEUCCI DEPOSITION)

"A man in my employment at one time, somewhere around 1849, complained
of being sick, and I thought to try electricity on him. He was placed in one
room, and the end of the wire being in circuit two rooms beyond his, I
went there wishing to know how strong a current I was using, and I had a
duplicate of this instrument with me. I called to him to put the copper part
of his instrument in his mouth. I did this because I had read that disease
could be cured [told] by electricity. The man, while he had the copper in his

mouth, cried out from the effects of the shock. I thought I heard this sound more distinctly than natural. I then put this copper of my instrument to my ear, and I heard the sound of his voice through the wire. This was my first impression, and the origin of my idea of the transmission of the human voice by electricity." (FIG. 2)

PRESET MARINE TELEPHONE MODE (MERMAID CHORUS)
Perhaps you should not
have told him that we use
electric eels to shock away
our headaches.

PRESET INSTRUCTION MODE
Keep your eyes peeled for pianos.
They are everywhere too.

PRESET ANTONIO MEUCCI MONOLOGUE MODE
Sometimes I sit in the square and score
the rainstorms—this one starts with
two boxes of Esterre's pins dropped one
at a time onto the drums, starting from a height
of approximately five centimeters, then
over the course of three minutes increasing
both the number of pins and the distance
between the pins and the drumhead. Soon
the rain morphs into a clatter of pencils in
the wings, then three men running up and
down the backstage stairs in heavy shoes.
I don't think the audience will even hear
the pins, but they may feel the neck-prickle
of a coming downpour. One day I will make
an onstage rainstorm so perfectly real that
a woman in the audience will forget where she is
and open her umbrella, a bright red flower
blooming in the dark field of the opera house.

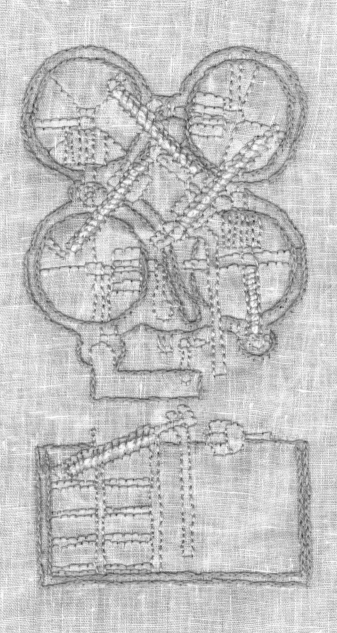

No. 122973 CORAL BLEACHING PROCESS

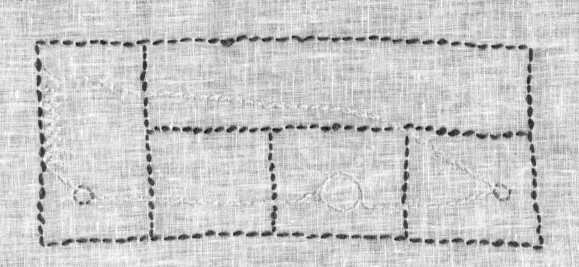

Fig. 2 TRANSMISSION OF SOUND THROUGH WIRES

PRESET VERIFIABLE FACT MODE

CROSS QUESTION NO. 339:

Why didn't you patent your speaking telegraph in 1860?

ANSWER NO. 339:

Because nobody wanted to believe it was true what I said.

PRESET MERMAID MONOLOGUE MODE (ESTERRE MEUCCI)

Humans, do you not all breathe the same
air? Yet you curtsey to that one, kick
the other. Some feet are slippered in pink satin
and carried over puddles, others bare.
When we arrived, they gave us a man to serve us,
as if he were a pebble. The theater is full of
invisible rules. White ladies may eat ice cream
on the right side of the patio. Chinese workers,
mulattoes and blacks sit way up high,
where the chandelier blocks your view, but
Chinese tourists sit with middle class whites.
Only the aristocracy is allowed in the boxes.
God knows where they'd put me if they knew.

PRESET STAGE DIRECTION MODE

Wheel in the mountains for Act One. Don't forget to oil them before every
performance—we don't want them squeaking like mice.

PRESET ANTONIO MEUCCI MONOLOGUE MODE

"When my telettrofono is in operation the parties should remain alone in their
respective rooms and every practicable precaution should be taken to have
the surroundings perfectly quiet. The closed mouth utensil or trumpet and
enclosing the persons also in a room alone both tend to prevent undue
publicity to the communication. I think it will be easy by these means to
prevent the communication being understood by any but the proper persons."

PRESET PATENT MODE

PATENT 46607 PROCESS FOR MAKING WICKS
OUT OF VEGETABLE FIBER (APPROVED)
(According to Esterre, there
can never be enough candles.)

PRESET PATENT MODE

PATENT 36192 SMOKELESS KEROSENE LAMP USING TWO
ELECTRIFIED PLATINUM PLATES TO EMBRACE THE FLAME.
". . . the flame obtains a great brilliance, more than
the gas, and puts in combustion all the oil that
is brought to the wick, and does not make any
smoke . . ." (APPROVED)
(I tease her, calling her my queen
of kerosene and she frowns,
saying, "I don't like queens."
Yet there she sits, a circle of lamps
like courtiers about her at all times.)

PRESET MARINE TELEPHONE MODE (MERMAID CHORUS)

Have you ever heard of an impoverished
mermaid? Pearls? We have shellsfull.
Treasure chests, etc. spiral down in slow
motion, bump softly onto the ocean floor
and spill their treasures. We don't know
what to use them all for, so we crown
the crabs, hand the octopus the scepter.

PRESET MAIN TELETTROFONO MODE

Antonio, will you bring me some seaweed
but please squeeze all the seawater out of it?

PRESET FAIRY TALE MODE

Once upon a time, in the time of
once upon a time, there was a mermaid
who loved sound and light. At the opera,
she was drunk on arias and candelabras.
But soon, as fairy tales often do,
the story would turn stormy.

PRESET MERMAID MONOLOGUE MODE (ESTERRE MEUCCI)

At first, in Havana, it seemed I'd brought
the luck of the sea with me. Those divas

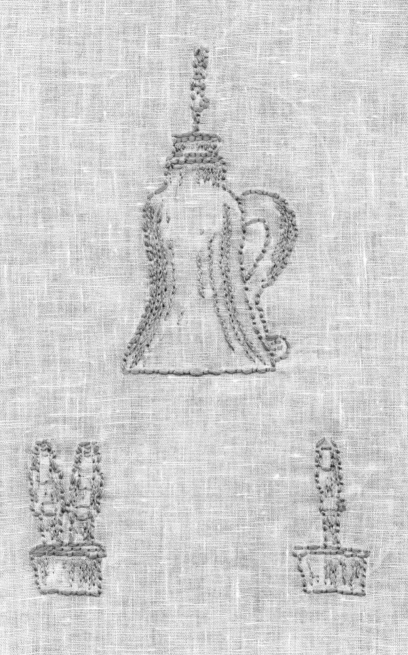

No. 36192 SMOKELESS KEROSENE LAMP

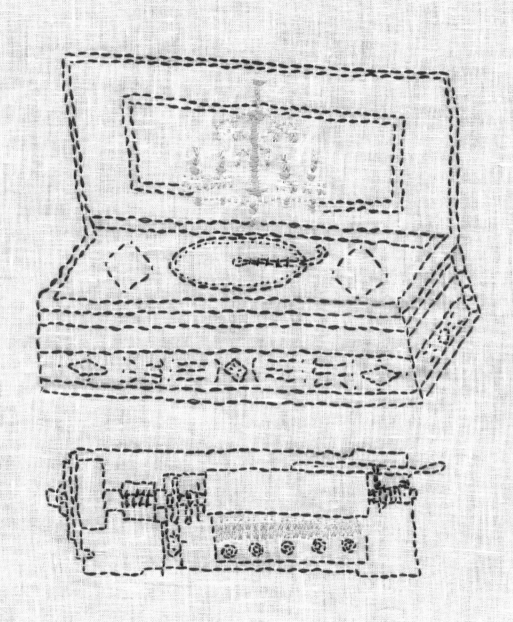

No. 170654 MUSIC BOX WITH SPINNING CHANDELIER

I sewed for were always winking and tucking
jewels (secondhand, from their admirers
at the stagedoors) into my pockets, certain
I'd make their costumes the prettiest.
People lined up outside Antonio's laboratory
to have their candelabras, buttons and swords
silvered. But that was while I was still standing.
The minute I took to my bed it all slipped away.
Of so much gold nothing is left us.

PRESET MARINE TELEPHONE MODE (MERMAID CHORUS)
Look at them now. They might as well
have minus signs on their foreheads.

PRESET VERIFIABLE FACT MODE
From 1838 to 1857, the Havana theaters produced 108 operas, 1,108 tragedies,
and 48 operettas, using 211 sets and 13,787 costumes. If the Meuccis arrived
in 1835 and departed in 1850, what percentage of these costumes and sets
were they responsible for?

PRESET VERIFIABLE FACT MODE

Whereas in 1850, Antonio and Esterre Meucci sail from Havana to New York and settle in Clifton, Staten Island. Whereas Esterre's so-called arthritis becomes increasingly severe and she is mostly confined to their second-floor bedroom. Whereas Antonio installs a telettrofono that runs from his workshop to Esterre's bedroom (FIG. 3), making a total of twenty-five different models. Whereas neighbor children call the Meucci's home the Devil's House because they know about the machine that lets voices travel unnatural distances. Whereas the Meuccis, not knowing how to speak English, are swindled out of their savings by a series of scoundrels and Antonio's various ventures, including a candle factory and a brewery, all fail.

PRESET MAIN TELETTROFONO MODE

Hello, Antonio? I need more candles.
It's underwater dark up here.

PRESET MARINE TELEPHONE MODE (MERMAID CHORUS)

Esterre, be realistic. You know
mermaids live to at least three hundred
and humans are lucky to make it to
eighty and then with awful turtle-wrinkles.

PRESENT PATENT MODE

PATENT 176432 PIANO WITH GLASS KEYS (PATENT NEVER FILED)
Shhh. Listen. I made that glass piano
back when Esterre still loved sound, but
last week, in secret, I sold it to a friend.
His daughter practices her scales almost
every afternoon, though not for long enough
if you ask me. She's good at the major scales
and a mess at minor. Most afternoons I wander
by to hear the slight crunch of the low F
(I left the edges a little rough on purpose).

I made the piano base from the roots of grapevines.
Each note tastes like a cold green grape.

PRESET STAGE DIRECTION MODE
Switch the sky backdrop behind the houses from day to night.

PRESET PATENT MODE
PATENT 176161 STAIRCASE PIANO—PART SOPRANO,
PART SEA CANARY (IMAGINED)

PRESET MAIN TELETTROFONO MODE
Antonio: Esterre, are you cross with me?
Esterre: No one wants for anything in the sea.

PRESET ANTONIO MEUCCI MONOLOGUE MODE
Sometimes I carry her up here for the quiet.
My poor Esterre, who once delighted in
each wheel-clang of the Havana train,
who clapped with the applause of
a whole balcony, winces now if I close a door
carelessly, if I sneeze. I tiptoe around
the house, but the slightest sound pains her—
she feels the clank of a cup in a saucer
(from one story up) as a knife to the knee.
The tick of my watch makes her wince.
Someone teach me how to muffle a factory,
how to hush the horses clattering by.
This is the only place where she will
unwrap her ears, and then only when
I signal to her that I have stopped
breathing heavily from the climb up the hill.

PRESET PATENT MODE
INDICATOR TO KNOW WHERE IS TO BE FOUND THE SHIP, WHETHER
S. N. E. W. (FOUND IN MEUCCI'S NOTEBOOKS, PATENT NEVER FILED)

PRESET MAIN TELETTROFONO MODE

Antonio, I'm lonely.

PRESET MERMAID MONOLOGUE MODE (ESTERRE MEUCCI)

Like his ideas,
the wires are
everywhere—
threading across
the yard, into
the basement window,
up through an
unused heating pipe,
swimming round
the stair banister,
seaweeding in
through the window.

PRESET MARINE TELEPHONE MODE (MERMAID CHORUS)

Your human needs an anchor.

PRESET PATENT MODE

PATENT 168273 IMPROVEMENT IN METHODS OF TESTING MILK
(APPROVED)
(Esterre requires that the milk be
precisely as creamy as when it came
from the cow—for her cats,
that is, and, if there's any left,
for our morning coffee.)

PRESET MERMAID MONOLOGUE MODE (ESTERRE MEUCCI)

For weeks now, I've dreamt about a silent theater.
No *soffitisti* chattering from up in the trellises,
so it's not the Teatro della Pergola, and it can't be
the Gran Teatro Tacón because the chairs are covered
in velvet. Mold bloomed so quickly in that climate—
a hover of green fuzz that only I found lovely . . .
It's no theater I've seen before. Each light is brighter

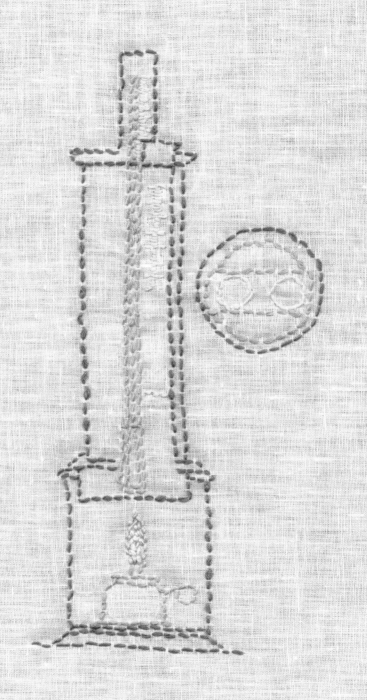

No. 168273 LACTOMETER

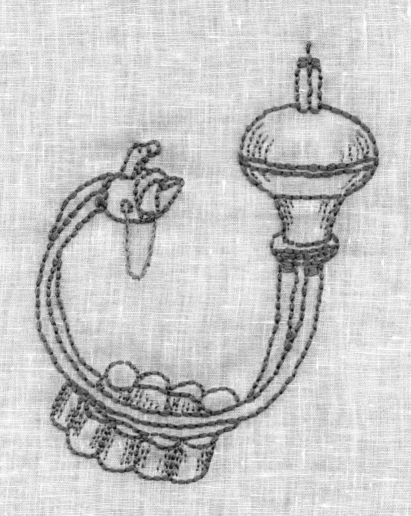

No. 369000 MARINE TELEPHONE

even than the araña chandelier in Havana, and that
had several hundred candles. These lights have
round flames and wires snake from them into
strange face-holes in the wall. What trickery
or forecast is this? Where is Antonio?

PRESET MAIN TELETTROFONO MODE
Antonio, the cats are hungry.

PRESET FAIRY TALE MODE
Once upon a time, in the time
of once upon a time, there was
an inventor who loved a mermaid
and would do anything to please her.
Because she loved sound, he invented
a megaphone, a telettrofono and a drink
that fizzed with the tiny effervescent
fireworks of fermented fruit. Because
she loved light, he invented smokeless
wicks and built a candle factory. Because
she was over-fond of candles, he invented
flame retardant paint. Because she loved
her cats, he came up with a way to carefully
quantify the amount of cream in their milk.
Because she missed her sisters' voices
he made a marine telephone. Because
her bones were not made for this loud
human world, they began to crack and
ache and crumble. Because she needed quiet
he tried to hush the trains, the carriage,
even the gulls. Because she could no longer
climb up or down the stairs, he carried her.

PRESET VERIFIABLE FACT MODE
House Resolution 269, June 11, 2002
Whereas Antonio Meucci, the great Italian inventor, had a career that was
both extraordinary and tragic. Whereas Meucci was unable to raise sufficient

funds to pay his way through the patent application process, and thus had to settle for a caveat, a one year renewable notice of an impending patent, which was first filed on December 28, 1871. Whereas Meucci later learned that the Western Union affiliate laboratory reportedly lost his working models, and Meucci, who was at this point living on public assistance, was unable to renew the caveat after 1874. Whereas in March 1876, Alexander Graham Bell, who conducted experiments in the same laboratory where Meucci's materials had been stored, was granted a patent and was thereafter credited with inventing the telephone.

PRESET PATENT MODE
MARINE TELEPHONE: WAY FOR THOSE THAT WORK UNDERWATER CALLED DIVERS HELPED BY THE TELEPHONE TO SPEAK ABOVE WATER (PATENT STILL PENDING AT TIME OF DEATH)

PRESET MARINE TELEPHONE MODE (MERMAID CHORUS)
Calling us "divers"
is probably a good idea.

PRESET PATENT MODE
METHOD TO RENDER INCOMBUSTIBLE THE WOOD OF HOUSE, CANVAS, ROPES, STARCH SIFTERS, PAPER, ETC. Its cost is very small so that every person can buy it and make use of it also in underwear, when it is washed in starching it with starch mixed with said composition in order to prevent it taking fire in case of a fire, or any other cases (PATENT NEVER FILED)
(Esterre is always leaning
too close to the flames.)

PRESET MAIN TELETTROFONO MODE
ESTERRE: Antonio, how are you?
ANTONIO: Will I make you some spaghetti?

PRESET MERMAID MONOLOGUE MODE (ESTERRE MEUCCI)
Of all the mammals, cats move
the most like fish. I love their fur,
soft as seagrass, their trilling purrs.

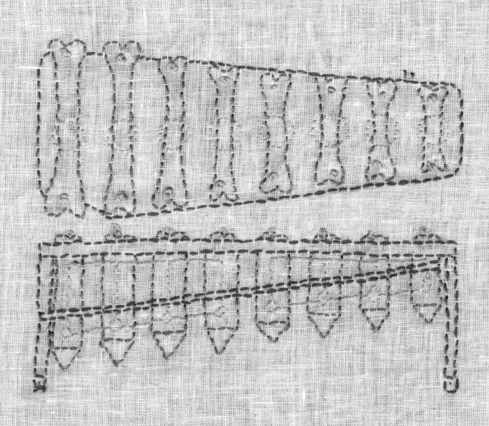

No. 169876 BONE XYLOPHONE

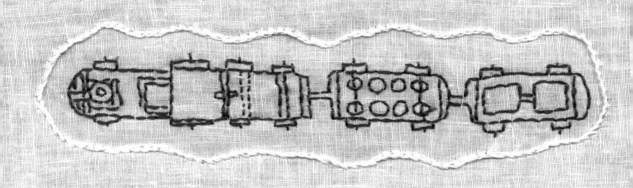

No. 370983 NOISE PREVENTION SYSTEM (FABRIC)

With my last bolt of velvet, I made fins
for my school of twenty-five felines.
I cut out fifty triangles, laid them out
on the floor, sewed them together,
stuffed them with sawdust. Three
of the cats bit me and bolted before
I could buckle the fins on. Lillina,
the old white one and Segreto,
the shy one hid under the bed,
but still, today I sent a school of
twenty sharks swimming down
the stairs to surprise my sweet Antonio.

PRESET MATH PROBLEM MODE

If a man living in Havana makes $30,000 (the equivalent of $500,000
today) electroplating buttons and swords and candelabras (spends $10,000
on failed experiments in human petrification, lends $200 to a friend) and
his wife makes $13,000, then they move to Staten Island, where he opens
a salami factory, a candle factory, and a brewery, which all fail, then receives
an offer of $10,000 to start a papermill using his newly patented paper-
making process but is only paid $75 dollars when the papermill goes bankrupt,
then takes a job at another paper plant for the sum of $20 a week and works
there for six months, files more than twenty patents and caveats for various
inventions including the first telephone, but is routinely swindled by his
business partners, and while he is gravely ill his wife sells his telettrofono
models to a junk shop for $6, what is the probability that this man will be
bankrupt on his deathbed?

PRESET MERMAID MONOLOGUE MODE (ESTERRE MEUCCI)

My fingers might as well be claws.
Yesterday, for half an hour, I tried to
thread the wrong end of the needle.
I saved up for the handkerchief
(even five cents is a hard sum to spare,
and I could afford only cotton, not linen),

wanting to embroider his other darling
—the telettrofono—onto it for his birthday.
But my stitches make me sick. They look
like the work of a drunkard or a child.

PRESET MAIN TELETTROFONO MODE
Antonio, my legs are hurting me.

PRESET VERIFIABLE FACT MODE
November 14, 1855, Antonio Meucci, letter to his brother
"All I can tell you is that I am in very poor circumstances and perhaps I have
to run away. All that I owned has gone, and all that I have left is the home
and the ground and the candle factory. But it is idle to talk about candles, as
nobody wants them. I have now started making pianos, but this business is
not doing well either. As you can see, I have no luck and everything I start
seems bound to fail."

PRESET MERMAID MONOLOGUE MODE (ESTERRE MEUCCI)
See that rock cluster there?
There. I used to hide behind one
just like it and listen to their
strangely immobile babies,
plump as scallops, screaming
and slapping the glassy sand.
A hundred hermit crabs waved
from the reeds. A human stomped by
in very tall shoes and the crunch
of his feet was a symphony.
But my bones weren't made for
this world and now each sound
is a knife to the knee.

PRESET PATENT MODE
PATENT 370983 NOISE PREVENTION SYSTEM FOR USE
ON THE ELEVATED RAIL (REJECTED)
(I tried it out in miniature—

No. 370983 NOISE PREVENTION SYSTEM (ROSEMARY)

No. 369881 SNOWCOAT WITH MATCHING MUFFLING MUFF

swaddling toy trains in cloth,
planting thick rows of rosemary
along the tiny tracks
to muffle the sound.)

PRESET VERIFIABLE FACT MODE

Deposition of William Rider (Bell/Globe trial)

CROSS QUESTION NO. 151: He was inventing something or other all the time, was he not?

ANSWER NO. 151: I think he was; there is not question about that.

CROSS QUESTION NO. 152: You considered him a genius, did you not?

ANSWER NO. 152: I considered him a genius at first, but afterward I considered him rather an impractical genius.

PRESET PATENT MODE

MARINE TELEGRAPH—FOR USE ON SHIPS; THE INSTRUMENT
WOULD SIGNAL SHIPS UPON THE WATER SO THAT VESSELS WOULD
NOT COLLIDE IN FOG AND STORM (REJECTED)

PRESET MERMAID MONOLOGUE MODE (ESTERRE MEUCCI)

The experiments exhaust me. He smuggles
me down to the shore at night and packs
my aching legs in sand or little mountains
of salt (no more electric shocks for me),
and though he looks at me hopefully,
we both know I'm not long for land.

PRESET VERIFIABLE FACT MODE

On March 16, 1881, the Meucci's cottage was moved across the street.
Esterre was quoted in the *Richmond County Gazette*, saying, "If it tumbles down I shall die with it."

PRESET MARINE TELEPHONE MODE (MERMAID CHORUS)

We know you hear what the sea is saying:
Come back or you'll crumble.

PRESET MATH PROBLEM MODE
In the case of the United States Government versus American Bell Telephone Co. and Alexander Graham Bell, which took twelve years and ended without a decision, there were 5,000 pages for the government's preliminary proceeding, 6,600 pages of evidence presented by the defense, 365 pages of government replies and 6,000 exhibit documents. What is the total number of typed pages for the trial?

PRESET ANTONIO MEUCCI MONOLOGUE MODE
If I could make her anything?
A staircase piano where each step sings
out a sound that is part soprano,
part sea canary or a stairquarium
filled with phosphorescent fish.
Coral fusilli with clam sauce.
Opera glasses that peer into the future
and under doors. A xylophone made
of our creditors' bones. A cat made of
limelight. A needle that can sew through
water, light and stone, the strongest seaweed
thread. A snowcoat to enclose her in
snowquiet with matching muffling muff.
A shell that purrs when you scratch it.
A music box with tiny spinning chandelier
complete with functional candles. A wave
metronome with interior surging ocean.
New legs. New legs. New legs.

PRESET STAGE DIRECTION MODE
Start cranking the waves. Rattle the tinsel wires for a slight smattering of rain. Tilt the mirrors so that light hits the stooped bearded figure carrying a woman wrapped in a blanket to the water's edge. Seagull cry three beats later, followed by flap of wings. When I kiss Esterre on her lips, then on each cheek, dim the lights, so the audience can only just see her slip back into the sea. Close the trapdoor quietly as the actress slips under the stage. Curtain.

Fig. 3 MEUCCI HOUSE, STATEN ISLAND

ACKNOWLEDGMENTS

TELETTROFONO

was originally created as a soundwalk with sound artist Justin Bennett for STILLSPOTTING NYC: STATEN ISLAND, a Solomon R. Guggenheim Museum project. Many thanks to David van der Leer and Sarah Malaika and all the stillspotting volunteers. The complete audio for the walk can be found here: http://www.poetryfoundation.org/poetrymagazine/article/247174

Much gratitude to the Meucci-Garibaldi Museum in Staten Island and to the late Basilio Catania for his indispensable three-volume work, *Antonio Meucci: The Inventor and His Times*. Other texts consulted include Sandra Meucci's *Antonio Meucci and the Electric Scream* and Giovanni E. Schiavo's *Antonio Meucci: Inventor of the Telephone*.

GIGANTIC THANKS

to the Kingsley Tufts Poetry Award, to the American Academy of Arts and Letters' Addison M. Metcalf Award, and the Jeannette Haien Ballard Writer's Prize for their generous support.

TO JEFF SHOTTS, Fiona McCrae, Katie Dublinski, Erin Kottke, Marisa Atkinson, Michael Taeckens, and the whole marvelous pack at Graywolf, and Sarah Gifford, this book couldn't exist without you.

GRATEFUL ACKNOWLEDGMENT is given to the editors of the following magazines, websites, and anthologies for giving a home to poems and artwork from this book: the Academy of American Poets' Poem-a-Day project, *American Poet*, *American Prospect*, the *Awl*, the *Baffler*, bombsite.com, *Harvard Review*, *Lo-Ball*, *Margie*, *Mermaids Magazine*, the *New Yorker*, *PEN America*, *Le Petite Zine*, *Poetry*, *Poetry London*, *A Public Space*, the *Same*, the *Sonnets* (edited by Sharmila Cohen and Paul Legault), *T Magazine*, *Tin House*, *Tuesday Journal: An Art Project*, and *Underwater New York*.

THE HOMEMADE MERMAID is for Mark Strand.

 is for Gertrude Rosebrock.

THERE'S A STRING ATTACHED TO EVERYTHING
is for Lisa Iacucci
with title thanks to Toby Campbell.

 is for Carol White.

LOVE TO
ROB,
WEDNESDAY,
VAMOS &
MEUCCI

HUGE THANKS TO MY WONDERFUL CORNUCOPIA OF COLLABORATORS

"The Straightforward Mermaid" was adapted into a short film, *Sea Full of Hooks*, by Ani Simon-Kennedy of Bicephaly Pictures and can be seen here: http://vimeo.com/23964968

Jeff Koons's illustration of "The Straightforward Mermaid" can be found here: http://tmagazine.blogs.nytimes.com/2013/04/10/a-picture-and-a-poem-the-naked-truth/

"M Is for Martian," an erasure of Ray Bradbury's "R Is for Rocket," was commissioned by Adam Shecter for a book that accompanied his show *Last Men* at Eleven Rivington.

Pre-whited-out photograph of Thai hula-hoopers by Sakchai Lalit/Associated Press.

"Woman Lives in House Made of People" was printed by 2-Up, a collaborative poster project. The drawing used on the miniature house photograph is by Monika Zarzeczna. "The Anti-Suicide Fox" was also a 2-Up poster, with alternate imagery by Adam Shecter.

"Inside the Glass Factory" was comissioned by the Poetry Radio Project, a collaboration between the Poetry Foundation, American Public Media's Performance Today, and the White Pine Festival, as a multidisciplinary performance of Philip Glass's *String Quartet No. 5* with the Miró Quartet. Audio from the performance is available here: http://performancetoday.publicradio.org/features/2009/06/poetry_glass/

"When the Water Is at Our Ankles" was comissioned by MOMA for the show *Rising Currents*.

"Last Stop Dreamland" was commissioned by Odyssey Works.

Paul Tunis's poem comic of "Game for Anything" can be found here: http://paulktunis.com/2013/02/21/game-for-anything/

Many thanks to Guy Pettit and Jono Tosch for curating *Words and Pictures Show* at Flying Object, a joint exhibition with Amy Jean Porter.

Pre-burned Kangamouse photograph by Adrian Kinloch for *Underwater New York*, which commissioned the poem.

OTHER WORKS BY MATTHEA HARVEY

POETRY

OF LAMB, with images by Amy Jean Porter

MODERN LIFE

SAD LITTLE BREATHING MACHINE

PITY THE BATHTUB ITS FORCED EMBRACE OF THE HUMAN FORM

CHILDREN'S BOOKS

CECIL THE PET GLACIER, illustrated by Giselle Potter

THE LITTLE GENERAL AND THE GIANT SNOWFLAKE, illustrated by Elizabeth Zechel